Portraits

self reflections in haiku

by: Twozdai A. Hulse

© 2017 Twozdai A. Hulse
All rights reserved.
Made in USA

First Edition

Library of Congress Control Number: 2017917912

ISBN: 978-0-692-98314-0

Photography, Cover & Interior design: Twozdai A. Hulse

Atrium Arts, LLC
Edmonds WA 98020
www.twozdaihulse.com

Portraits
self reflections in haiku

by: Twozdai A. Hulse

Forward

I started writing haiku in my early 20's and have not looked back. Before you take a step inside, you should know, I've never had a strong sense of punctuation or proper grammar... I let all of that go as I write Haiku.

When I learned of Jack Kerouac's style, "pops", it spoke to how I was writing. I was not writing in the traditional sense of a Haiku, rather writing poems consisting of 3 short lines - quick sketches that roughly fell into the 5 | 7 | 5 pacing .

So of you are a stickler for rules, you will probably find the following pages a bit like nails on a chalk board - but if you can let go and see them as quick snapshots of to create a visual portrait through words, you might just find little pieces of me on the page.

Haiku's from 2002–2017

Thank you,
Twozdai

(p.s. Twozdai is pronounced Tuesday)

Gratitude

To Penny, Dorothy
& Cathy, words are to small
to say I love you.

Thank you Carmen
for going on this Haiku
journey with me.

There are so many people
in these pages and in life,
to offer my thanks.

Today and always

in case I forget
to say, you are amazing
and well, I love you...

let these words find you
and remind you, you are worthy
beautiful and strong.

you are not alone.
you are seen, you are nurtured
you are loved.

xo t

Post holiday traffic blues

back in the red sea
miles of winding tail lights
the slow swim home.

Winter

snow is deafening
In a way that rain can not
even imagine

More please

Sunday morning
a pocket of ripe tomatoes
woodpeckers and chai tea

Just sayin'

You know what doesn't
Go on top of your toothbrush?
Fancy face lotion

Weekly rituals

sheets and blankets - clean
corners tucked, cover smoothed out
the perfect made bed

Goodbye 2015.

you said you love me
I might have imagined it,
just the once, as you left.

Is this week over yet?

I'm just too tired
to do much more than laugh.
thank god it's friday.

Choices

Oh Chocolate,
my stress adores you, but my
pants no longer fit.

Not everyone agrees in here.

My heart would like to make
an official complaint to
my head and gut.

"You might be right, but
I stubbornly disagree...
at least for today."

This old routine

date night with yourself
fancy dress, sexy hair, Manhattan...
home by 6pm. boo

Fall storm

driving in starlight
the roads littered with branches
dinners on camp stoves

Monday, I want to love you.

some days feel like
a long road full of pot-holes
in a rain storm.

All in a days work

Winter gardening
cleared out some blackberry's
& caught a bug in my eye.

Sums it up.

Falling asleep, you realize
Your underwear has been
Inside out, all day.

Aweigh

City parking lot
Lined with industrial anchors
We aren't going anywhere.

Old friends

dripping in moss
the old forest reaches
down to the river

Before the day begins

It's quiet in here
Early mornings alone
Me and a heater.

Hello cars

Walking to work
Feels a lot like playing frogger
Today I won!

How is it only 1pm?

Red sky's in morning
Bring sailors warning...
True for designers too??

Goodnight

in memory of Christine

You were the first,
the wise one with a smile
our older sister.

its too soon.

Friday morning

Back to back meetings.
Two coffee tastings before noon.
Corporate speak overload.

The fence blew down

Without power
24hrs and counting.
Good thing I like storms.

It's too damn early
(good kitty)

Woke up to mouse catch
Kitty wants to play not kill
I want to sleep

While you sleep

A long hot shower,
quiet walk in the garden,
kitty killed a bird.

This week

4:45pm
Hello spinning beach ball of death.
I just need one file ...

House guest

I hear you up there
scuttling about above my bed,
you were not invited.

Gratitude

Thank you fear for showing me
the things I most care about.
Now stop fucking with me.

Surrender

Resolve is my super power
Sometimes its my Achilles heel.
Today I surrender.

Lessons between us

You teach me that
People are better than no people.
I'm still learning.

Surrounded by your people.
The only one who can let me in
your circle, is you.

From the sidelines I believe
Even when you can't see it, I believe
I don't cheer, I believe.

So much noise & nonsense

There is stillness in quiet,
an opening in mindfulness.
Who gave my brain candy?

Summer storm

Midday lightening.
Sky rumbles, windows battered.
My sentiments exactly.

Car break in.

glass scattered about
Dirty laundry is missing.
I hope you're my size.

7am, waking up.

the snow does not melt
seagulls call across rooftops
quiet morning view.

Perspective

Oh, that's a tiger.
I thought, maybe a brothel?
A zoo you say?

Spring stories

A tea kettle blows
Dancing across the breeze
Through open windows

Is the moon afire or flooded?

This spot right here.
I tuck this one away for me.
With out ownership.

Shoreline

Your heart shifts like the tide.
My heart fortified with walls
that are breaking down.

Hello & Goodbye

Sunlight through the blinds.
I trace your collar bone to remember,
the negative space of you.

The positive space of "we".
my head on your shoulder,
tucked into the now.

Shift, flux & pull.
We both know, only the earth
can take on the ocean.

So here we sit
Two types of fire alight.
Mirrored and at odds.

When you call the moon, expect your heart.

The black wolf guides me.
afloat on the calm waters.
Black wolf is angry.

We near the shore,
Stag waits for me at the edge of the wood.
I must leave black wolf.

Dressed in constellations,
I follow stag into the woods.
There, I take on his skin.

I nibble the grass.
hearing a rustle I know,
To be strong, I must die.

I feel wolf stalk me.
I resign to my fate.
to die, is to live.

....

Falling through the dark.
Laying naked in the boat.
Afloat in the unknown.

I pull on the coat
of the white wolf - she's the moon.
eclipsing my stars.

Rain

seriously
I have to peel off my pants.
No more puddles.

Soft moments

Curled up and stretched out.
Mountains move in a soft breath.
Piercing eyes and smirks.

Late night musing

Here are the cross roads
it's not surprising, really -
my hour, your month.

A dance

A run in with past
A tango with forgotten
A waltz with before

A knowing of now
A salsa in a passion
A wanting of more

A willing of calm
A want of complete balance
A dance of two.

If only

To forget the moon.
To ignore the night sky light.
To be that easy.

Sometimes I am at odds.

I want to run trains
into the ground till they stop
or just plant daises.

A little ice and cold

Snow bound and stupid
I'm not prey to your follies,
I just wish I was...

Maybe that is a lie
pride is such a funny thing.
I do like the play.

Thaw

wet cheek against cold
fingers. the heater takes a long
raggedy breath.

It's cold in here

my heart beats against
my rib cage against the hard floor
that is your ceiling

I shot a gun.

This is me with a
a revolver in my hand. It's
not pointed at you.

Or pointed at me.
Yes it's loaded, but really,
take the bullets out.

Morning

Fogs sleepy blanket.
Suns greedy hands pull at it,
to warm our cold skin.

No regrets

Morning walk of shame,
my bra and poetry books
tucked inside my purse.

Snack pants

These brown corduroys
They remind me of first grade.
Jungle gym fever.

Horse races

Dressed for the races
watching the horsed go round
bets come up empty.

Deep pour

the night dips away,
glasses of wine, empty,
and yet we linger

Temptation

I think about you
I shouldn't think about you.
But there you are.

Fly on a wall

A night out alone,
ease-dropping on your first date.
Can't say that I'm impressed.

We can be change
(Nov. 5th, 2008)
tonight is the night
a night that we shall transform,
a night to believe

Plot lines

A werewolf walks in
to a bar and says to the
wooden spoon - we're one

....

I've read too many
vampire and werewolf stories
and too much Robbins

Could you owe a spoon
your eternal life and more?
would you even care?

Early Morning thoughts

foggy halloween
its easy to imagine
zombies and ghouls

New Scents

my boyfriend smells like
banana coconut run
while on vacation

Maybe it means something

applying on-line
as an internal candidate
keeps being denied.

Out to Sea

after a spot of tea,
I think of him, with row boat,
Victrola and cat.

Driving into it all

in the freedom, the
compact capacity of
this city, I'm home.

They stole my battery

6:30 is to early
in the morning to find your car dead.
Bastards took my battery!

I'm going blind

looking for glasses-
I wonder, who's your eye doctor-
forward info please.

Last night at Sonar 2006

my feet have worn out
i watch a girl dance in pure envy
I used to be her

I'm not always good at waiting

I'm HUNGRY
Deliver my Thai lunch NOW!
did I not say please?

An ode to the Internet

Before my coffee
till I turn down my sheets,
I turn to you-dear internet

In Memory

*It's hard to wrap up all that you feel of a person in one haiku,
so I give you a memory my meeting Ephraim.*

You grabbed my hand and
reminded me to dance, not
just on the floor, but in life.

Stranger

I want to believe
that he gave me drink & flower
of his own accord.

the cynic believes
on a night like tonight,
he was sent.

Before my eyes have woken

Golden strands of light
filtered through arms of a tree.
Still sleep in my eyes.

Scientific study

Curtis eating
chocolate for us, does not
fix our cravings.

Powerbar undies

there's performance food
& performance underwear-
not to get confused!

Now

its been 6 long months
since I've put paint on a brush
tonight I'll smear it on heavy.

Haiku Driving

Amber alert!
something went missing
today

Work and such

I'm practicing my hissing skills
its come in handy-starring at my computer
things I wish would go away.

Your fur is sprouting

Oh moon pull—
the werewolves are itching
under the skin

No haiku

I have the hiccups,
they drive me crazy,
make them stop-please

Warming my engine

its a skirt day again-
this may be a short lived trend
my knee caps shiver

Amen to that

Hello old friend weekend
I wait so patiently five days in a row
to celebrate your freedom

I said my goodbye-
(shh, don't tell them that I cried)

Yesterday was safe
tomorrow is full of change
step, step... jump, splash - swim

A collection of untitled Haiku.

summer breeze came in
as fast as the winter chill
left us paralyzed

"No Parking" signs line
a road which traffic sits still.
Parking by default

how can a Tuesday
feel like a whole week has past?
collapsing hours.

a walk to the park.
My attempt at working out
I should run 5 miles

so long mary anne
a good song for this morning
chai, Leonard, haiku

one thing I learned was
I am a mother bear
there are more lesson's

to be a hello,
there has to be a goodbye
razor sharp, dull edge.

the animals play
on the roof above my bed-
squirrels playing marbles

crows feet & laugh lines
a natural part of aging,
tell me, why the zits?

my bed freshly made
I should easily find sleep
but words win the night

a fond weathered key
hard to imagine its use
being so tiny.

there is no jungle
no mountains or plains to trek
just an old book shelf.

perfect winter scene,
blankets of snow wrapped around
an unused air stream.

amongst the decay
of winter passing through one
leaf lingers in fall

I leave at 9am
for San Francisco, and I
haven't packed a thing.

city lights sprinkle
down with the late night rain
just me and a bus

eyes barely open
there's a quietness in the city
just these flowers stand out.

dancing flys
weave & swerve in time
to afternoons song.

floating bicycles
all of them I'd like to ride
but instead they fly

rose left on sidewalk
now sits in a glass on my desk
I keep trying to drink it.

morning message brings
what you call my small smile
simple delights.

I fill my in box with
distractions. little hamster
wheel running.

languid notes cut sharp.
smiles break up at me,
a night not yet warm.

Searching apartments-
when I have no real reason
to relocate

excuse me sir-
I've run over your haiku,
today's misfortune.

a bike abandoned
on a desolate gray street.
no rider wanted.

the list is ten miles long
of things I'd like to do &
things I have to do.

I could curl up in
a sweet ball of deep sleep
in less than 5 min.

you wait for tomorrow-
oh, darling, I wait for no day
well maybe lost days.

is love chocolate
flowers, champagne & kisses
or smaller moments?

stories shared of
innocence, love & regret
to open ears.

my piles of books
stare at me, wanting a home
up, off the floor

is it little things-
all piled up to once continuous thing,
or just over thought coincidence?

The things we learn
in the echos of each other-
I'm glad he's my friend.

"I suffer for my art"
but more often - it suffers
under my weight.

these nights, these dreams.
bleeding together, fading lines
blur reality

today I'm listless-
who stole my motivation?
I'd like it back, please.

crowbar in the wall
the history of these bricks
waiting to crack away.

this is no haiku
but I've never claimed it
to be more than a pop.

the 11o'clock bus.
your shuttle down to me-
teleport please.

resolutions - well
I quite disagree with them.
I grow all year long.

dressed to go out,
in the style of a librarian
still at home

hard to break old habits
even knowing they are - well old
staleness lacks flavor

morning donut–
glazed & playfully sprinkled
yummy in my tummy

I want to perform
29% over last year, 17% over plan
in my personal life, not work.

it's time I make it clear
I'm not your back pocket girl
things must change.

I'm looking for a muse,
maybe you can be mine-
we could create together

Today I have to let go,
Tomorrow I have to let go,
when can I hold on?

today was a day
for driving to the ocean
letting the waves catch my toes.

the old houses with their stories
the old chimneys raise their smoke
the newness settles down.

piano keys echoing
deep emotional strings pulling
resonating hearts

give me a dance floor
& deep, full beats-
I'll give you my soul

Black & white images
catching plain moments
making them rich

Sitting in the cold
at my piano
releasing on the keys

Taking it in - letting it out
balance
I guess is the goal.

His body curled the length of mine
I lean in - in comfort
and squirm in excitement

standing naked
nervous fidgeting paused
in full exposer

some days I look down
and see my mothers handwriting
on the tip of my pen.

post-it note haiku's
my desktop escape &
doodlings

its funny what time
and age bring with them
& leave behind

I refuse to forget
all those moments that we shared
laying in my underwear

It's more like my mind
has not slowed down in 2mo.
time to shift gears

a stranded sequin
it's lone friend on the floor.
project from months past.

I worry about you
I try to free my mind
but you seep back in

eyelash on paper
a piece of my sight
left unguarded.

I pulled the blinds down
I pulled my clothes off
and fell to bed

its Saturday I'm awake-
the sun was up just before me
I'll be up long past it.

"embrace this RIGHT now"
embracing should be of love
not urgency.

there are lessons here-
floods of them pulsing by,
just reach in and pick.

on one hand I'm biding my time
on the other, I'm exploring
the depths of me.

I don't know how to
do any of this gracefully
but I'll do my best.

your little red truck
worn down by the years—
and holding your youth

car under attack
the tree throws its seeds in protest
to such a presence

radio tower
reaching up to call the sky
a patient protest

His truck is named tank
he moves it only half a block
and retreats again

east side caller
jolts me from my gentle sleep
with no explanation.

possible thumb print
places me at the crime scene
of my writing.

rain falls on the car
engine idle, radio plays
a song to forget

deep jazzy beats
set to be a reminder
of your hearts pounding

It's a tight spot were
my heart lets go these days
its wants are it's pain.

Contact knitting
almost came into play today
one sharp comment short

a cat in a hat
no- she's go her head stuck in
a tissue box

spot of tea and cards
sunny Sunday at the park
slowly taken in.

from sun to Fog
this bridge takes me in to the
disappearing city

tip-toeing threw early morning
responding purely to instinct
rather than thought

as time moves forward
its the circular path
that brings us back

every Sagittarius
I know is a homebody
with social butterfly ideals.

she peaks out behind
her mothers blue hem, as if
it was her fault

Just when I'd stopped looking and
given into the unfortunate luck
you stroll up.

slow rising morning
I want today to stay asleep
tight in a lovers arms

its a long dirt path
scattered with freshly fallen leaves
leading outward and inward

Pocket my heart
here's your window
of opportunity.

red light, red room
I kissed Colin in that hall
many, many moons ago.

I find myself
looking for your junkyard heart
on the roads of mischief

I'm holding him,
against you - his memory
still haunts and holds.

she walks up-
sniffs, meows, stretches
and leaves.

standing at dark gate
sign says no trespassing
unknown, we go in.

in the arms of night
standing on the widows walk-
the house seduced me.

The normally soft
light of morning has turned harsh
on this old kitchen.

dusty rays of sun
only increase the feeling
I'm in a Brautigan.

Soaked in hot sunlight
feet push against smooth river rock
toward the waterfall.

surrounded by
the crash of waves and the
roar of a train.

Things I saw and liked:
wood airplanes and broken trains
in a dusty sunset

I say I am hiding-
all the time I really know
I am being found.

walking the dock towards
strangers turning into friends
paintings and sleepy eyes.

I should take that advice
to stop before its to late
but not ride the brakes.

If forgiveness is
possible, would I let it?
trust and respect gone.

I ran into you
only on paper but still,
I ran into you.

todays horoscope
predicts a calming effect
I'd very much like that.

Dali meets hopper
my dreams are interpreted-
and then translated.

indie rock driving
guitar rifts on auto pilot
drumming out the day.

My car stopped today.-
I'm stranded again this year.-
Can I be done now?

today, slow to wake
socked in by the grey fog
softening edges

We recognize each
other, by painting, by thought
crow vs monkey.

removing the threads
of the life I started to weave
recycled yarn.

its been a long day
I turn my phone to silent
and take in whats real.

How many more walls
need to be built in protection
till love is lost.

Chocolate lips, sweet scents
I like how he holds my hand
sugar tongued moments.

Warehouse open—Night train
the same rush with out the sand
again I follow.

Long night, toss & turn
to watch each minute tick by
eyes close, alarm sounds.

standing on the stairs
where Kerouac once lingered
amused by the change.

the web I've woven
sticking firmly to my past
I try to shake loose.

its not tomorrow
or even my yesterdays
that can hold me in.

grey paint on my feet
remnants of inspiration
traveling with me

The ocean calls me-
her energy in my blood
I move with the tide.

econo-christ,
even your name entertains me
cheap religion

My gato negro
sweet red wine warms my belly
like a black cat hug

My eyes express more
than I ever mean to say
and more than I feel.